EXCEEDS US

LEAH POOLE OSOWSKI

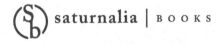 saturnalia | BOOKS

Distributed by Independent Publishers Group
Chicago

Saturnalia Books
105 Woodside Rd.
Ardmore, PA 19003
info@saturnaliabooks.com

ISBN: 978-1-947817-54-8 (print), 978-1-947817-55-5 (ebook)
Library of Congress Control Number: 2022947292

Cover image and book design by Robin Vuchnich

Distributed by:
Independent Publishing Group
814 N. Franklin St.
Chicago, IL 60610
800-888-4741

For John

The room he brings into you
the room befalls you

like the fir trees he trues her
he nears her like the firs

if one vanishes one stays
if one stays the other will or will not vanish

otherwise my beautiful green fly
otherwise not a leaf stirs

—C.D. Wright

CONTENTS

I.

TEMPORALLY   3

WHEN THE SEVENTEEN-YEAR CICADAS ARE DEAFENING   4

AMONG   6

ADORE, DOORLESS   7

MEETING, REPEATED   9

CHURCH STREET   10

SLOPE   12

LIKE A GILL BECOMES A SCAR   13

CONDITIONS OF AIR   15

CONTROLLED BURN   17

THERE'S URGENCY   18

WITHIN THE BLUE HOUR   19

II.

MOTIVES AROUND HUMAN VACANCY   23

VS. FIELD   25

MAKE YOU A LAWN, FIELD, SIDE YARD   27

IN OUR FIRST HOUSES   29

LOCATED   30

STILL HOUSE   31

PUPA   32

LISTEN, THE CLOUDS ARE MOVING NOTICEABLY FAST   34

SO BELOW   35

III.

WHICH INFINITY   39

EXCEEDS US   41

PURGATORY   43

REMEMBER THE STRANGERS, THE LIGHTNING, THE WRECKED AFTERNOON   44

UNCLEAR, THE LEVEL OF THE TIDE   45

MUTED, MUTATE   46

THEIR EFFECT   47

THE WOOD, A HERD OF COVES   48

HARD AS APRICOTS   49

IV.

WITH AN EAR TO THE EARTH   53

SOMEWHERE BETWEEN FULL AND SPARK   55

IN THE KINGDOM   57

CUMULIFORM   58

THE ALTERNATIVE   59

SURFACE TENSION   60

V.

VERNAL   63

MADE HIM A LAWN, FIELD, SIDE YARD   65

THE WORD *RECURSIVE*   67

THE WEEK AFTER YOUR RETURN   69

PHYSIS, PERSIST   70

FIRMAMENT   72

ADRIFT WITH SHIFTING LANDSCAPES   73

PRIMARY, PRIMAL   74

A KIND OF AMBULATORY PASSAGEWAY   75

PARING THE EARTH   76

VALLEY OF THE GODS   78

MOTIVES AROUND OBJECTIVE REALITY   80

DOMAIN: EUKARYA   82

I.

TEMPORALLY

How you can occur in two places at once. How the ocean
alters pale green to light-lost gunmetal. I had no idea this capacity

existed, until the sky exposed its huge dry self.
Unobstructed. The sway between rooms. Ballet of tenses.
A decade, a swarm of mayflies, cast skin,

light intensity their cue for emergence.
The solar eclipse in totality. Two-minute night. A ring
in the ears. The way we're only one dimension

away from time travel. Oh, imagined life.
I slip you over my forearms like ice. The hind leg of a grasshopper
mid-bound. Portals open and shut like riptides.

Shores recede. Sandbars in the mouth. I want to change enough times
as to be hardly

recognizable as mammal.
Sweet fin-legged future, with your salt skin and baleen teeth, beat me
against the reef, force a different mode of breathing.

WHEN THE SEVENTEEN-YEAR CICADAS ARE DEAFENING

Say she's a road
                    with no streetlights.

A knee-deep sink step into marsh.
A caesura pond.

And a month is a plane flying west through time zones.

Unpeeled nights
                    still on the stem.

Low tide recedes a mile.

We can walk across the bay but the bluefish
will chase us back.
                              Hamstrings bruised like ripe figs.

We see with fingers that grip the shirt in front of us.

A tadpole coughs out two legs.

                    The shortest distance
                    between two places is running.

Remember when the storm rounded
the point and her hair stood on end?

She bottled that charge, sips it on days with flat fields.

She spits bluffs
and we don't know if we're being deceived
                        or given a sand cliff to jump.

Because black water is   a different species of swimming.

And sometimes we don't know

                        if our eyes are open or closed.

AMONG

I said I fear the Pacific but they're all the same body.
The way we all breathe the same air
                                        eventually. Gulf Stream, Santa Anas,
Spring Creek and sweat that pools under the eyes. Aren't we all astonished

by where our minds confront us when left alone with an open window?
There's no limit to this high season.

The decks are packed and people line their backs against the walls like cutouts.
We could be anywhere
                             with a view. Waterspouts, a dim alarm,
a white crane flying
                       impossibly slow.
Or ponderosas sloughing their vanilla skin in ribbons. Gibbous moon
                                  the ball of the thumb to moor teeth marks,
      fairy circles in the field of the palm. I'll carve an ocean
in my hip bone, live a different sea a day.
                                      You, shore here, and John, your
                     dimension, there.
Who told us we had to live one life?

ADORE, DOORLESS

Stone floors rope the night

      The bay a hoof print

                        a green bite mark

Skin something to cool in

Windows as garnishments   knifed aside

      a curtain a winged thing

The language of ice in glasses

                      dilating a room

The raft   its own island

The beds   a longer version of float

The distance between   water and sheets

             negligible

Stairs optional as steps

            Stares as steps toward

What's spurred in a long gaze

            has muscle here

has uncaged

paw at the glass doors

Four legs   line up   on the railings

pounce stance   stalk-and-ambush

Tension is the thing with feathers

Extremity: as hand   as boundary

as magnitude

MEETING, REPEATED

His hands are too soft, they unbind me.
Oscillations in our chests, Richter scales

behind our foreheads, we meet
and repeat, glance and lateral.

This is the reef and look how bright.
What I mean is: when the giant tank

at the aquarium is gazed from three different
levels, through three different glass panes

of varying thickness and concavity,
the perception of held water and millions

of scales is distorted. As are the angles
of approach to encountering a new *you.*

We're ploughing each other out at what depths
and who will leaf out of the caves—

chests the yellow of greens gone to wilt,
mouths the repetitive *but* of the moray.

CHURCH STREET

A small fish pond clicks
beneath the giant sycamore

out your bedroom window.
The ocean across town

rushes back. I rearrange
your room, center your bed

so we can orbit as we learn
the pull of each other.

You visualize white blood cells,
biologically immortal jellyfish,

our lives on loop. I run
the neighborhood against

its current, choke on magnolias
and planula. They say change

is futile in total return but
I'm sweeping the mayflies

off your deck and cutting onions
towards their cores. I'm testing

my new gills for walks
in the shower. I'm standing

knee-deep in the brack
of your voice not thinking

about eels winding my calves
as the sky's overtaken

with starlings. Just that
the word *murmuration* exists.

SLOPE

I rush the room of your mouth. Like opening
a hill a flock of more grass so I roll down.

I am inside and outside of myself:

I see you see a girl in your plaid flannel trail a stick against a brick wall
declining toward a river. Her hair traps the solar hour in strands
of redwood bark. The shirt is a basket of soil.

I see myself, cluttered and still with tail, carrying spent years
like stacked glasses tucked between chest and arm.

Imagine the most arrant shattering. Shards with high exponents.
All I want to do is keep my months out of your fingertips.

Keep you wine-hilled parked on a brick street in a June downpour.
Hook the right mix of rain to knee-slide down the banks
of each other, unstained with all our skins intact.

LIKE A GILL BECOMES A SCAR

Amphibian means *two lives*
they drink through their skin
mouths closed   I fill

John's water glass past
the top   he lowers face
sips the rise off the rim

Below the table under his
skin is a kidney from his
second life   his first

plays rugby in the field
tackles ghosts
grass-stains air   reckless

are bodies
before they're taught
to break

Spiders skim
the pool showing off
the miracle of cohesion

Six legs are a lot to keep
track of   But how often
do we inventory limbs

Another frog drowning
in the skimmer   his
chlorine trance

Exhausted   John's
first life dives into the
deep end   tadpoles

in circles   showing off
the strength
in his one flat tail

CONDITIONS OF AIR

Slowed is a summer with five speed bumps
        to keep our wheels grounded

keep our toes stubbed and blood-blistered

Naked
        the rose-less road   All the fences
        undressed   your scar a cross-
        beam on your abdomen

All the light
            pinpricks and laced

The lots wear clothesline necklaces
beckon
        in hydrangea

Bed spreads thin as a letter opener

Walls envelope night-sconced voices

Pines tuck needles
        under mattresses like teeth

Fans oscillate in every room

In every room
       someone occurs
       remembering

Floors sweat like foreheads

Knock the curtains down one more time
       and the tide won't rise

Every time someone's tricked
       into the screen door

they hit turbulence   in another life

CONTROLLED BURN

You tell me you used to tape your ears playing rugby and I think of band-aids snatched on the pause between two and three. I think drywall. I think of all the ripped intersections of an animal consumed. How last week we hooked black tip sharks seven miles offshore and didn't think about the way their lip, cheek, sinus felt at our pull. And you congested for a month because you lack an immune system. Because your single kidney is existing in the pause between two and four. Because there's food chains and organ chains and silver chains around my neck that keep breaking links. Remember the human knot at summer camp—how a pile of hands gripped and contorted towards any direction that wasn't letting go? If I ripped down the posters in your childhood bedroom two holes would be revealed where your fists tried to wrest free of the collapsing building of your body. Decay that came in through the ear and slowly weakened the core. I remember my worst ear infection as a kid: watching Scarlett O'Hara return to a burning Twelve Oaks. A plantation fire in my cochlea. And you five states away—cornfields smoldering, and refusing dialysis is running straight into the bear-filled smoke. Red rover red rover. If I could I would throw those sharks back, I would stop the filleting, stop the pelicans spitting out tough skin, stop the jaw from drying propped open on the deck, stop the ungrasping, and turn the fire in your yard into a prairie burn.

THERE'S URGENCY

In a stairwell   how quickly a church
is engulfed by flames from linseed-oil-soaked rags

This crosshair look on my face is called rush
because between you
                    lacks oxygen and stained-glass

The idle of first days:
          empty swimming pool window
          clomp of horse on brick a hollow
that folded the surface
          of non-water into corduroy

Snap green trees awning the deck   hours
stretched out like deer hides
                    a crawl-speed undoing

It's not how long you stay in my life
                    but that I be with you for yours

Perspective flipped like a prayer kneeler
my bruised-plum knees

We tie red thread around each other's wrists
begin and again and for how

WITHIN THE BLUE HOUR

The ginkgo leaves like thousands
        of folded fans, and we needed them
in the new heat. June finally acting her age.
In the dusk, the fox lopes the lawn at its diagonal
jumps the wall, his mouth full
        of feathers. Hold your breath
to keep his pace.
John upstairs stops tossing his sleep,
        wings plucked from the air.
Peonies slaughtered by rains.
        Algae like so much silk
        in the garden pond, a bullfrog
pushing his throat in labor.
Three half-filled glasses on the stone wall
        to catch and hold, to keep the yard kept.
The small girl takes five tries to remove the word
exoskeleton from her peach mouth. Last night's
        feather still threaded in her hair
        picked from the pool where a flock
        of ducks just died   unexplainably.
Bamboo stalking the brief woods.
                One bee
on the floor of the pantry, its breathing caught
by yesterday's full moon.
My whole life I searched for love like clover.
        Honey removed
                from the bone.

II.

MOTIVES AROUND HUMAN VACANCY

Boketto (Japanese, v.): gazing vacantly into the distance (without thought or sense of self).

How windows do   how cows do

How a parachute blooms calm
slows motion
                            a house of corner-less sky
            a round to rove in

How you wake in an unfamiliar bed
                no idea where here is

Or how one wakes after another's death
and for five seconds they're not

This white space   this difference
between snow and seeds
                                    and the way they drift

Or steam and cold breath—
the simultaneous distinction and confusion
                            of temperature

Clarity translucing
                                    the way a cloud covers
the sun causing the ocean
                        to put heavy clothes back on

How Nebraskans describe the air
just before a tornado:
      green and shock still

             mouthing *cellar*
             mouthing *chance*

VS. FIELD

I could stare down   a field

but it has distraction

Collapsed deer   swoop of hawk

lightest stumble of monarchs

my eyes   adulterous to this lake
of grass

The wheezing rye field

The fox a flare
next to the broken-down car of me

Give the wind a leaf   and dare
it to keep still

Dim the lights

and beg the cicadas silent

Movement

and noise take

        no instruction

Thistles   still draw the foot
still defeat   the callous

Cry thorn
and see the skin creek

Cry splinter   and invite
        the outdoors in

MAKE YOU A LAWN, FIELD, SIDE YARD

I'll mow until the light bruises, until shards
of grass erect fences in my hair to keep you home.

The neighborhood fumed with the green
alcohol and aldehydes of you.

You faint stain—skid of mantis—under fingernails
edged scrapes.

You, the earth waking, stretching acres,
resuscitating my inert horizon.

How many hours saw you upright on your father's
riding mower, layering your lungs, ragweed, bahia.

Shearing patterns into grass—rows and crosshatch,
you, cleaning up land,

the downhills, the lines that keep a girl barefoot,
keep her rolling your slopes, dew-damp and perennial,

blowing grass blades between thumbs, rubbing wrists
into sod for an honest scent,

because you as ground are meant to be worn and stalked
and breathed like sweet vernal grass.

Because it takes a back pressed to the earth in exertion
to approach the brink of sky.

IN OUR FIRST HOUSES

You wake to field, tree line, mountains bent over whisper *texture*
to the dirt. Your bedroom window a hectare green.

I night to branches, dusk deep anchor blue of whales,
my rectangle of glass five feet off the floor. My outside angles up.

Yours—three stories down. Our acute opposites.
My favorite color: a tired sky. Yours: a half stadium crowd

of hemlocks admiring the mow lines in the grass.
I see Pleiades and the veins in my thenar a drowned map. Your iris—

a roots-eye view of sycamore. *Darse un verde de algo.*
If we could exit this atmosphere, reduce our ground to a globe,

perhaps we'd wonder who favors white—the thick cocoon web
of weather patterns yelling *transience*, yelling *vantage.*

LOCATED

his handwriting, a flock of seagulls
we're riding a free ferry

              the wind a herd of horses
we're standing on a 700-foot high dam, we're clearing
our plates, we're backlit

              and blacked out like alcoves
the water could crush a house

        the water you could walk on if a small girl asked
we're spelled-out

            incantations, canter in the backwoods
overgrown, gowns on, overblown

            the wind a sloth of bears
look at my finger
tip up, grass blades in the nail

            the wind a high dive
      water barely split
his handwriting, a loose stone wall

           dynamite in the mid-seam
we're warranted

      watering the interstellar dust,

                mooned, marooned
we're very high up and the wind

      the wood, a herd of coves

STILL HOUSE

Removed from the porch
the plants played arboretum
by the east window.
The field saged with first frost.
The ones asleep wore socks.
The plants adjusted their leaves
to vented air. The sleeping ones
reheated the air with absent breath.
Their bundled heels. Their suffocating
arches. The roots rooted around
in too small pots. The crack of toes
muffled like seeds in pulp in pods
on the honey locust. The mattresses—
docks of soft wood. The stairs go up
trying for a better view of the mountain.
Their descending version is looking
for groundwater. They all look for ground
and water.

PUPA

A deer hangs on the guard rail like a beach towel

the last word hangs on the air like a drenched tent
        no sleep in the woods

The mint in the fields   a prelude to juleps

The weekend wetting its lips
                in the near future

With miniscule top teeth   the fox wet their burr-
matted paws
           underbites like halted steps

Exuviae in the bench vise and there will be a show

Heads on pillows   heavy as rotten grapefruits
         migraines whisper   *here comes the parade*

The light across the rye lengthens   pupils stretch
circumferences   like inkblots born in pockets

       Did you say earlier you were born on a ferry?

Like velvet rope barriers on a floating dock

the rooms sway to the faint smell of yeast

                    and browning gardenias

The day a ship chugging between two points

               Ahead   an island with a tallest

Behind   a porch wraps around the house

                  like arms that won't let go

A balcony   the second to last sentence

        caught in its throat

LISTEN, THE CLOUDS ARE MOVING
NOTICEABLY FAST

creek so dry it hurts to swallow.

wind shifts under our skins, maps out its far-off autumn.

browns the alliums to ghosts.

thistles soldier the perimeters, thorn us in.

the town next door mistakes rabid grey fox for coyote.

shoots the whole skulk. drone of highway scrapes up our sleep.

I never fished alone because of the hook removal.

almost impossible to believe some things don't have nerves.

touch tongue-tip to elbow and no one was there.

your second face slipping out the back door of your face.

how walking on the balls of feet may or may not be quieter.

think of the authority in a heel, a thundercloud.

the rain in sheets like your third face, running out the front door.

my response time like borer bees, their hover.

if I could feel every bone in my body I'd panic at the inventory.

in emergency, I'm drywall, useless as a stare.

time wrapped up in a cloth cloud, wool thick, wedded.

a scream just red hibiscus, blooming out my mouth.

SO BELOW

The hawks lie on air

                      coast their loops. We float in the pool
wave our limbs slow like surrendered squid   push off the sides and glide in lines
for as long as the air in our lungs will let us.

                              You wake me
with the proximity of your face   tap of focused pupil. I would know you
in someone else's life, someone else's storm cellar.
Freight in the sky. Tunnels in the lawn imploding.

                      A hawk dives into a hemlock, disappears.
Its wing breeze stops the clouds, reverses their direction,
rewinds the stranger's kidney clean out your gut,

                           the renal failure locked under bulkhead.
The eye of the storm no longer

                      your eye that wakes me in half dark. The other half—
hawk's white breast   clean as new life   third chance.

III.

WHICH INFINITY

Two rooms, connected by balcony, shared interior wall
        almost the same view

The same blue hour opens the day but is nothing like dusk

An outstretched palm receives a heavier weight than expected
downward compensation,
              slight drop in some version of horizon

In this case
        she couldn't stop looking at his hands, unwavering

sculpting landscapes of air
fingers long as the shadow of the house across the back lawn
            and over the bluff

Trees full of apricots
           her hours full of pits

To hold desire and evenly consume the sphere of it

How not to get caught
           in the ending

evening   of rocks large enough

for sitting and empty stone streets

evening of seeing through the one shared wall

the first deep breath will take you the whole length
of the pool, underwater
                                        and the quiet, the wavering
light   the no need
                    to emerge

EXCEEDS US

Their spines   eastern redbuds

      Open their fists and a frog kicks perfectly
           down the depths of a green pool

Hear the creekrush in their raised voices
      see the light undo between the branches
               in their pupils

Her favorite sound: a two-hands rock dropped
          into still water

His last dream: the landscape not land at all
      every direction electric blue water halfway up the trunks

      Tree bodies so slim you could cup your own elbows

Count the circles in the largest stumps, two lifetimes
      in a minute

A century passes overhead in the shape
      of a Steller's jay

      That color   drowned heaven
      half-dipped   prominent crest

a head the waves would envy if the waves were here

They beak each other's necks
        roll in a line then foam the hard sand

This isn't about approach   heaving   bent waists
                            a call and response
        It weighs less than that

This a story of retreat
        deep where blossoms
        calcify into vertebrae
                        murmurs beyond the larval stage

PURGATORY

Months so full of bees their mouths
coated in pollen, their touch sting-heavy.

The sea glass-bottomed and loaded
with submarines. They linked elbows,

formed human chains for the wind drills
its cool touch felt through the larynx wall.

Hundreds of strings vibrating on all different
instruments. They wore their newborn eyes,

half there, half before; the earth transparent,
you could see straight through the core.

Magma in a white-blue dress, her iron-nickel
knees. The layers deviating and the light

barely shut off at night. A planet
up for interpretation. They quickened

like pontoon boats in their hot metal skin,
their thrum preceding their bodies, their roam

imitating the word *while.* Their length of time.
Their even though.

REMEMBER THE STRANGERS, THE
LIGHTNING, THE WRECKED AFTERNOON

Withheld, they woke the storm, boarded
the boat and eared the hull to hear
how sound travels through saltwater,
if it too feels buoyant. Who are these us
in this bright green sea? Slaughtering
light, it licks their calves and hooks a strap,
stares down their undertones. Half-naked
they sit on the cushioned benches, absorb
the wake and skiff, the motor a dozen
moans, these barrier islands bearing
witness to what? Their relocation,
their getting-to-know-you town, their first
weekend to an outlying island, crowds
of cordgrass, sawgrass their edges, to where
wouldn't you do? The anchor drifts,
the tide de-escalates, boat beached
and showing white thigh, they walk the path
to hear the sand, ghost crabs bury the daylight.
The storm defrosts, squalls the wail,
arm hair a thousand needle-rush, fresh-cut
postures, dumbstruck girls, pray the day
forgets their faces, prey to wide-open rides,
thunder-fueled and lightning devoted,
how similar—trawling and almost.

UNCLEAR, THE LEVEL OF THE TIDE

Look at me. A turning away from the mantel.
Map of the island's inlet covering the wall. By map, you mean photograph.
The blues deepen in knots. The gulf of crossing a hallway.
On the porch rail of dangling legs, they focused inward toward welted light.
Backwards, the sound dipped into her grasses. Pelicans in V's
the water-weight sadness of every August, every alternative
not yet lived. Fluorite months with triangular faces.
On other bays, it's impossible to see people outside the circle of firelight.
They stack bodies in the sand, the darkness cool on their eye beds.
Talk of hip bones as doorknobs; talk of tan lines your salt bed.
Walk through the house, thumb the latches, unlock all the windows.
Crumple the thin paper of your parameters to flame. Chimney flue:
sooted future, turning of the damper, sparks rising all the way up.

MUTED, MUTATE

Boarding the rowboat in shadow bodies,
the light, everywhere in tongues, except
on them, and ears positively ringing
in insects, muted pastels, pasted shore.
Steady, ineffectual as a goal, ghosted by
the marsh and her mood swings, the water
snake's tendency of effortless division.
One of them weighed the day, bagful
of nectarines, the other measured monthly
progress of the sun yolking the horizon.
Their sluice-blue hearts irradiating their
chests, they spoke heron in undertones,
oar-lock in the pauses, until a thunder
overhead, an all-consuming decibel
escalating atmosphere and the hearts
climbed their jet-fuel-coated throats,
slipped out their mouths, tranced
as bucket carp, drifted straight down
to mud-depth and detritus, a split-decision
to estivate for a spell, burrow torpor and set.

THEIR EFFECT

John takes her hands, places them on his temples. *See?* The vein pulses under her fingertips, she pictures storms just formed in the Gulf, unnamed, repeating their rotation on the radar. If she pushed his head underwater could she cause a tsunami? Nights she dreams of them as a calm, five-story wave at the shore of a perfect beach. She thinks of snakes throughout a day, her scaled peripheries. She tells him of her reptile preoccupation, her eyes on his forehead, now a bedspread of skin covering a cold-blooded coil. The next day a thumb-thick, bright as new-growth grass snake falls from a tree onto the road in front of him. *That's the way she goes,* John says. She scratches a nail up her calf and the creek that winds through the county runs dry.

THE WOOD, A HERD OF COVES

The timber dam in her torso
starts to rot, her wrists rivers, forearms flood

with storm surge, otters collect at the elbow
seek cartilage to chew, an eddy

to carousel, her reservoir pelvis still as a deer
in high beams, until it lights in the hooves

finds the air off the field that drifts straight back
to brush, every bone a fell tree, every vein

a log flume, her horse trough mouth
goldfish swim among teeth, suck the algae

off her palate, forehead the first-frost
lawn, the damp receding from the east

she rips off an ear, lights a tea light
floats the pair across the bay of lost ankles

every plea heard, a goat drowns
in the flood, every yes, a girl steps

in a bathtub, dares her foot not to adjust

HARD AS APRICOTS

She floats above the well again   whispers
of an uprising

                    coaches the mimosas
                    in counterattack
a firing of leaves
recoil reversed

The crabapples projecting
strengthen their stems

                    evolve beyond a fall

cornstalks
rustle in pattern   a marching

                              in the field
Groundhogs widen tunnels
                    beavers reinforce forts

She turns over every
stone to incite small riots   collects bark

for armor   kneels under the laurel
palm full
          of bullets   teaches mimicry
          to fireflies

A river rock added each hour to the pile beneath
the bed
        a copperhead
                to the one against
the door

At night the oldest snake
curls around her calves
              warms his scales
on her brass
          paints her teeth
            with his poison
a last defense
      if they get past the thistles
      if it comes down to neck and mouth

IV.

WITH AN EAR TO THE EARTH

The dam retains the flood,
just as days harness the bodies,
keep them from thrashing wild.

We drive by a house built
over a creek and wonder
how often its tenants press

an ear to the floorboards,
eavesdrop on the speech
of flowing water—

ice, the unspoken,
and melt, the rush of rot.
Last night we saw a movie

where a man loses three
small children to a flaming
house, and this morning

I read a book of poems
where a man lets go his
wife to fifteen months

of leukemia. The quick
and the long but still dead.
Grief, like so many species

with different speeds and
strengths, wild and domestic.
Consider: someone walks

into a river, chooses
drowning, as another's
torn away in a flood.

Do both look at the water
they drink every day
and ask, *How could you?*

SOMEWHERE BETWEEN FULL AND SPARK

We split a lemon these mornings: hot water   alkalinity
                    a searchlight in empty stomachs.

The drive to the lake revealed a lack of lake
a drained space
                    like holding the bowl to your lips and tipping.

The drive through the woods to the abandoned church
revealed a haunted.
                    The low-angled sun couldn't quite reach
the boarded-up windows.

The white German Shepherd couldn't quite
                    ask us to leave.

The coals in nearby fireplaces cooled gray. Full is not always
hot light but we like to think it is.

I wonder if bones spark when they break. If on the inside
the bruising is a smudge of ash.

                    These days we're trying
to hold all our pieces together in our thin skins.

It takes extra tensing of the cartilage.

Every limb a river, every barking white dog a flood.

Like repairing a dam. Solidifying the arch
to distribute the pressure of the water to the walls.

IN THE KINGDOM

Fogged mornings   malaise of air
sun diffused   and tenuous

I always thought I had space
inside my body   pockets between

organs   like unlit rooms   But
anatomy speaks   of mesentery
a connective tissue

And suddenly I am solid   Or maybe
the fog has entered the house and

is touching every object   reminding
them they're one part of a larger whole

CUMULIFORM

John was crushing clouds against the hill
looking like snow but just the sky

assaulted. Pummeling
for rain for lightning for every plane

that never landed. For portals
for effortlessness for time paused.

Because he wants to be weightless
and white. Covering or awed.

Composed of nothing
but water. Organless.

Not this swollen ground
of conditions. Twice-daily swallows.

How can we separate
ourselves from our broken

bodies? We rape the landscape
we can see, start with what covers the light.

THE ALTERNATIVE

Instead of jumping in she asked
the water to rise up. Infiltrate.

The side effect of transition lenses
is they keep the light out of the eyes.

Rape became too harsh of a word,
but I wanted to use it anyway.
Rearranged, a pear appeared
on the table, mild green bulb.

I laid on my back, placed the fruit
over my heart, considered its sweet weight
with something other than hands.

SURFACE TENSION

As it melts, snow
plummets in chunks
like doves. The moon
is overfull.

An otter splits the marsh
and we forget our lungs.

Malena says walk over
bridges with moving
water beneath to bring
labor,

live moated, to discard
the body completely.

VERNAL

The equinox passed
two equal halves

unnoticed. Day lined up
back to back with night.

Spring measuring their height
with her thawing hand.

Twelve hours tall each
and then a swell of light.

Coaxing buds and bare legs.
Pollen a tongue tip drug.

Crocus throats thrusting
through dirt, cicadas

turning seventeen scream.
Nine o'clock geothermal

blue. Your lagoon hands
holding anything they can get

their heat on. Dusk
a dish thrown at a wall.

A wall a row of poplars
overpopulating the yard

you can't stop sleeping in
twenty Junes from now.

MADE HIM A LAWN, FIELD, SIDE YARD

I find grass blades in the sheets
green as ripe buds, shards discarded

like stray hairs. Then stains, clover-colored
shadows on the insides of John's clothes.

We bend two hours in the yard, picking up sticks
and inside the rooms have that just-cleaned look.

I stare at his hair full minutes and swear
there's a rustling, like someone removed

the lay of their body from his lawn.
John's bruising in yellows, all remnants,

as the field erupts in dandelions. Ghost press
of thumbprints on the insides of his limbs.

In a month, I'll blow the seeds off his skin
and wish for rain. Try not to imagine

the nightcrawlers digging through the dirt
of him, drowning in his mud. For now

I keep quiet, run my bare feet down his legs
as he sleeps, cut across the dark backyard,

just out of arch of the motion floodlights,
wake up dew damp, the sprawl of his back to mine.

THE WORD *RECURSIVE*

                  sounds out
from the podium and I picture script,
attached in loops, repeating.

But she's speaking science, buoyancy,
hot gasses, a lifting up.
                      Compromise
hangs from a clothesline, that weightless
drag of cord, faded open sleeves.

We've been jump-roping furiously
since the New Year, trying to acquire
tap-dance feet and crossovers, how to exist
in a quick orb of our own velocity.

The chant of whip and pavement, the thin
authority of wrists.
                How many fingers
have circled your carpus,
touched thumb to middle,
looked up with ownership
                    or something lighter,
                    some completion.
I've been taking breaks
to count my breaths, in sets of ten. Aware

of each its own hallway, its own up and back.

The word *poppies*, circled on the page.

Upward force, equal to displacement.

Your sore forearm,
scrawling letters on a fitted sheet, the bed afloat,
its very own island in air.

THE WEEK AFTER YOUR RETURN

We found a fox pup dead
in the middle of the field,
its entrails an untied ribbon,
buried it in brush. Hours
later, its mother burnt
our daylight perimeter
bright orange with sprint,
a frantic felt in the chest—
her looking: its own
wilder animal. My current
state is somewhere in her
flank, taut and bounding,
or her tracking instinct,
not knowing where or what
or how high all of this fell from.

PHYSIS, PERSIST

Tell me you've sucked the sap
straight out the tree trunk.

Tell me you've knelt knee-deep
in leaves, undressing. Tell me

of the copperhead that can't
dislodge your name out its throat.

Tell me you've stood oval
under whale ribs, begged to be

taken, a new dimension snapping
time like a sill-dried wishbone.

Tell me you shed years
like exoskeletons, and dear reader

please tell me you understand
the shape of a life and how many

we live is always negotiable.
Tell me you've measured lightness

by the stride of your sprints,
the catch of the chest muscle

throwing its shoulder against
the wall of you. Then tell me

the weights, the sinkers, are cyclical,
not an always for the heart

that needs a focal point
as in compass as compress

as a soft wet cloth against the skin.
To heal and to hold, to draw out

with the mouth a snakebite,
its name stuck in the lips of you.

Tell me unpoisoned, tell me in maple,
pointedly, or tell me in storm surge

with astronomical tides.

FIRMAMENT

My long skirt sounds like a gaff-rigged sail
between my calves and I don't know
how to leave this sky. The desert always
airing different versions of itself, removed
the audio from my voice. It glassed me.
The Apache plume exists as the translation
of flight into plant. Take my body, boat me.
Tack me toward a headwind that's daring
dry heat to lay down. I want to place all
my altar stones on your cloudshadow.
I want to blow my body to pieces for you
to scatter like milkweed. It's not worth being
whole when so many beautiful places exist.
Give me everything all at once and I'll water
your blue all drought. Teach me how
horizon is optional, and I'll tattoo your color
across my cold front. This spun world.
Grasshoppers and balconies, assembling
astonishment. I want to be the blast of air
you can't help but steer your face toward.
I want to be the language of dustbowl
hands when voices are torn from throats
like extinguished blue flames.

ADRIFT WITH SHIFTING LANDSCAPES

Postponed evenings,
days I can feel my bones as ladders,
propped but not leading elsewhere,
each glass of water a lake we haven't
yet visited, your foyers of voice still
someone else's house, and the leave-
less trees up the ridge like thinning hair,
a standoff with a buck, his companion
invisible until they bolt, minutes you
thought you had a handle on suddenly
unwrapped, opaque. This shipwrecked
life. Sea-lost. But isn't it gorgeous?
The blue. The salt dried on your skin
like a high tide line, the horizon a hem
on a closeted dress of some pretty
young thing just beginning.

PRIMARY, PRIMAL

Mars so red in the western sky, how could it not give life?
Like the face after five sprints, ruddying its blush out,
color that proves to the earth, yes,
                    I can move across you with speed if I must.
Like the barns, just standing there, staring.
Confident in their role of multiplying lives.
And your sister, parked in the driveway one night, years ago,
ceaselessly honking her horn
                    as three mountain lions did their pacing,
muscle muscling in the taillights,
the red now focused on a species so brutally honest
in intent that her face must have drained of its color.
There's a rumor that our blood is blue inside our bodies,
            but the truth remains red, the confusion lying
in wavelengths of light penetrating the skin with different
degrees of success.
Essentially, life is taken so other life can endure.
                            This part makes sense.
The ripped-open field fox does not,
                    nor how my whole life, on walks,
I'd wrench a beach plum or some winterberries off their stems,
just to feel their light roundness, before tossing them aside.

A KIND OF AMBULATORY PASSAGEWAY

At the party, a rat snake sheds its skin
the handler wraps the hide around his neck like a scarf and is taking
pictures by the windows.
                          The owls in their mews barely
focusing their twilight eyes as a crab ball rolls under a table.
This morning my car was covered in winding trails and the birds
          in the white pine gave no indication of snitching.
          A poet at the party says the word

                          circumambulate

and I remember the last time I saw the rat snake
          she had coiled around and over and under herself and I
          wonder if it's possible for them to knot their own bodies.
I wear a red string about my wrist,
                          tied in seven knots by my love,
but it has not wound the tomb of Rachel and we know no prayers.
I do know, some snakes can see the infrared wavelengths
          our bodies emit, and if I could, I would knot my legs
          seven times around my lover's heart
          if it would help him feel less weight
                          in almost everything,
I would cloud our eyes blue, slough our skins, withdraw
          before our past lives became someone else's
                          talking point, another's accessory.

PARING THE EARTH

To count the wildernesses, the haves
and have nots, the baby cobras

on long, brandished lawns,
tectonic verandahs; the shade,

that comparative coolness,
between memory and photographs,

water and none. You spent a whole spring
in the bathtub because of how far

the ocean was. Away.
A way of constructing small landscapes.

The windowsill: magpie feather, dried grasshopper,
clay bear with lightning scarred back,

brain coral from a recently bereft island.
Thenar-shaped sea glass, middle swamp

green. The bird of paradise
you tote house-to-house because it starred

in a movie and showed up in your unlocked
foyer at dawn. How in seven years

it hasn't bloomed but he told you it's a white one
and perhaps the thought of—

that elusive rarity, or the quick glimpse
in the grass, perhaps that eclipses the have,

the other halves, for now.

VALLEY OF THE GODS

Utah roads wind long and I want to place
my forehead on their mesas cliffs, quantum tunnel our way into Arizona.

Lay physics down and slowly undress her.

    Ask her how long it takes moving water to form natural bridges
    when a river takes a shortcut through sandstone, abandons its meander.

Tell her how we drove out to the dugway, to three miles of carved switchbacks,
    graded dirt clinging cliffside

and I swore the world had reached its edge, become a mass I wanted to get low
and cling to like groundcover, like gravel.

    Tell her how my body has a way of asking to stay earthbound—
    when it feels like an underbelly, or a cloud passing over an inner thigh.

Confess that we backtracked 100 miles, chose sagebrush over sky, for the grip.

    Decided against eroding into air.

And imagine her turning to me, like thunder but with an ear pressed against
    the floor, how she shifts a quiet landslide,

hands me an extra ounce of gravity to swallow
whispers, *you have your whole life to defy me, why not take it easy tonight?*

And I sleep like a dead jackrabbit on the shore of Lake Powell, held by the edge
of time zones, for now, exhaustedly human.

MOTIVES AROUND OBJECTIVE REALITY

Anitya (Sanskrit n.): Impermanence; the notion that existence is transient, evanescent, and inconstant

Like monarchs lighting up sidewalks that month. I'd hush *Mexico*,
remind them not to stay. The slight step of oranges.

There's a younger version of myself I'd like to drown in a river.
An older version whose arrows and aim I need to borrow.

How bait balls are the exact intersection of beauty and terror
and every decade we get to live a different life.

August, we watched the blue-sky rim of the shore birth cloud spits.

Prove how weather is not a god and I'll believe in you the rest of my life.

Shocking, how we're labeled and named as the same human
when almost every part of us regenerates.

Dear cerebral cortex, you are the stranger in the house.

The first visit of the season, we'd approach the beach unsure
of who she'd be. Her restless, erosive sandbars of identity.

Dear summer, you should be a law of science that never wanes,
blue and overfull, mouthing *slack tide,* mouthing *sure-fire.*

There's a woman in this town with one kidney. On her other side—
the imprint of a deer lain in grass.

Dear John, you're never anonymous in our story, I'll love you in blue
when these countries recede underwater.

Ask to ashes and us to dust.

DOMAIN: EUKARYA

Wolf throat, words pace
but don't exit the mouth.
                    The man in the office
across the hall is going bear hunting this weekend.

All I want to do is jump on the bear's back
and keep my eyes closed forever.

Yesterday I saw twelve deer at various times,
in different places. They lounge like underfed models
                            under the super moon.

I'm trying to understand time as non-linear.
                    Lord, make me a tree
so I can shed half my mass in color.
                    Exist in a perpetual circle.

In a dream I still bring friends home to sleep
in my mother's king bed,

or my dead grandfather still sits in the cottage
and no one knows why steam rises from his chair.

                    I'm trying to invoke a life
with an animal instinct.

Like running towards the woods.
Like climbing a tree as an appropriate response.

      Two dead birds off the porch this week.
Mistook glass for sky.
I admit, I love the muted
                thump their bodies make on impact.

But kneeling in the dirt, I line them up, apologize.

Their yellow-tipped tail feathers
                so bright they shame the sun.

I cannot believe in this life that gutters a winged thing
                          such as this.
That bullets the wild.
Momentum removed for a dull thud.
                    I spit the wolf out
and he tears toward every direction that isn't forward.

I spin the cedar waxwings
                like limp bottles
      looking for any aim to put my mouth on.

ACKNOWLEDGEMENTS

Grateful acknowledgement to the following journals in which some of these poems first appeared: *Alaska Quarterly Review*: "Valley of the Gods"; *Cimarron Review*: "Still House"; *Cincinnati Review*: "Vs. Field"; *Epiphany*: "Within the Blue Hour"; *The Georgia Review*: "Unclear, the Level of the Tide," "So Below," "Paring the Earth"; *Gettysburg Review*: "When the Seventeen-Year Cicadas Are Deafening"; *jubilat*: "Vernal"; *The Journal*: "Hard as Apricots"; *The Massachusetts Review*: "Domain: Eukarya"; *Mid-American Review*: "Controlled Burn"; *Ninth Letter*: "Firmament," "Temporally"; *Passages North*: "The Week After Your Return"; *Poetry Northwest*: "Motives Around Human Vacancy"; *Prelude*: "Muted, Mutate"; *Seneca Review*: "Exceeds Us," "Purgatory"; *The Southern Review*: "With an Ear to the Earth," "Primary, Primal"; *Sugar House Review*: "Listen, the Clouds are Moving Noticeably Fast"; *Zone 3*: "Among," "Pupa," "Which Infinity"; *ZYZZYVA*: "Remember the Strangers, the Lightning, the Wrecked Afternoon."

"Muted, Mutate" was written after a Marcus Dunn painting.

Immense thanks to Timothy Liu and everyone at Saturnalia Books. And in memory of Linda Gregg, her measured quiet, her ritual, her holy.

I'm grateful for Interlochen Center for the Arts and the girls of cabin 11; for *Image* and the Paul Mariani Fellowship at the Glen Worskhop in Santa Fe, Carolyn Forché and her 2017 class; for the Vermont Studio Center Fellowship and the writers and artists of March 2018, and for Jon Davis—thank you for spending time with this wind chime manuscript. To Penn State Altoona for the Emerging Writer Residency and the students of my 2018 class, thank you for that time and space. Thank you Steve Sherrill, Lee Peterson, Todd Davis, Julia Kasdorf, and Abby Minor. My gratitude goes out to Melissa Kwasny and Mary Ann Samyn for your own words and your poetic generosity.

To my parents—my world is greener and wider because of you. Thank you. Thanks to Alden and Janet for this love of words and books; to the Pooles, the Osowskis, and the McSheas. To Mar Mar, Addi, Kaylee, and Dax: the world is yours.

I'm heavily influenced by my landscapes: Brewster, Massachusetts; Boalsburg, Pennsylvania; Sea Isle City, New Jersey; Wrightsville Beach, North Carolina, these poems are yours.

To John, you permeate these pages. Thank you for being.

Leah Poole Osowski received Saturnalia's Alma Book Award and is the author of *hover over her* (Kent State University Press, 2016), which won the Wick Poetry Prize. Her work has appeared in *The Southern Review, The Georgia Review, Ninth Letter, ZYZZYVA,* and elsewhere. She earned an MFA from the University of North Carolina Wilmington and was the emerging writer in residence at Penn State Altoona. She is the poetry editor of *Raleigh Review* and lives in Pennsylvania with her husband, the writer John McShea.

Also by Leah Poole Osowski

hover over her

Exceeds Us is printed in Adobe Garamond
www.saturnaliabooks.org